How to Survive in College

A GUIDE FOR Confused Students

Francis L. Gross

UNIVERSITY
PRESS OF
AMERICA

LANHAM • NEW YORK • LONDON

British Cataloging in Publication Information Available

Library of Congress Cataloging-in-Publication Data

Gross, Francis L.
How to survive in college : a guide for confused students / Francis L. Gross, Jr.
p. cm.
1. College student orientation—United States. 2. College students—United States—
Conduct of life. 3. Study, Method of. I. Title.
LB2343.32.G76   1988   378.198—dc19   87-29025 CIP
ISBN 0–8191–6751–7 (alk. paper)
ISBN 0–8191–6752–5 (pbk. : alk. paper)

Table of Contents

To
Tori and Liz and John
To Jamie and Joe
To Priya and Raj
To Matt and Ben and Ed
all friends

CHAPTER ONE

On Campus

I am writing this book for students who have found college campus a confusing place. I am writing it for the people who don't know what to do rather than for those who know exactly where they are going. I am thinking of my own youth when I showed up at college not knowing anybody at all, in a college that seemed a million miles from my home, even if it was not that far. Being without friends was something that could be remedied, for there were other kids at my college who didn't know anybody either, almost all of them. We made friends all right, even if it took from September until Christmas for most of us.

But then there was that awful choice of courses; clearly somebody expected you to know what curriculum to be in. It was easy enough to sign up for something, but it wasn't easy at all to find a course of studies that fit what you were interested in. How do you know what curriculum will fit your interest? It took me a long time to find out. I hope it doesn't take you as long as it did me. But that brings us back, doesn't it? I am writing this book for students who find themselves in a foreign land when they come to college. I do not have a specific student age in mind, for I know that college students can be searchers at seventeen or at thirty-five. There is no specific age for being lost. You can be lost at any age.

I will admit that I am thinking of students who are lost, but I am thinking as well of those who hope to get found. I am thinking of students who think, "There's something out there in college some place that has to do with the way I will spend the rest of my life. It's out there, but I don't know how to find it."

Put another way, this is a book for college students who don't have their shit together....yet. There is a marvelous quality of expectancy about a great many college students,

1

especially beginners. I think of it as being a little bit like Christmas Eve. You don't know what you're going to get Christmas Day; you have hopes and dreams, but you just don't know yet. So, the air of expectancy and exasperation with waiting. Something holds you there on Christmas Eve; that's not the night that kids run away from home. You stay there to find out what's coming tomorrow....with your hopes and your fears. You just have to stay to find out....but you still don't know.

I think of college as like a very long Christmas Eve. Those who have no hopes at all, well, this book is not for them. Those who know exactly what they are going to get; I'm not writing for them either. If you don't know what you are going to do in college, if you hope that there really is something there around the corner that will be truly for you, then this book is for you...and I hope you read what I have to say all the way through. Mind you, I know that there are an awful lot of people looking. I know that besides being a lot of you there is a great variety. There are many different kinds of people who have that same quality of being searchers, the quality of being lost and not yet found. This book is not going to give you a blueprint. I don't know what the answer is for you. What I hope to do is not so much to give you the answer as to give you some good ways to search for the answer that will differ for each of you, because each of you is unique. There's nobody else in the world just like you. Still, there are ways of looking that may fit a lot of people. There are certainly a lot of common things about the world of the university in our country that we all share.

The world we live in is a fast moving place; at least it is in most American schools and in most American cities. To the beginner, at least, things move fast in a university. You have to be at class before you know where the classroom or building is. You have homework before you have managed to purchase the textbook. You have a midterm exam upon you just about the time you think things are just starting. The course is over before you know the names of the other students in the room...and then all of a sudden there is preregistration and you don't know what courses you want to take next semester, because you haven't even figured out the ones you have right now. And then there's the dorm; you never saw your roommate before, but you get to know that person FAST; you wouldn't believe how fast.

Should you stay in the dorm or move out at the end of the semester? If you move out, where do you go? All of a sudden the fraternities and sororities are rushing. Do you want to become a Greek? Which one? There are religious issues. There are moral issues. Should you cheat? Is it wrong to sleep around? How about getting drunk? Is there a God? Do you have time for Him or Her even if there is? How do you handle your parents? They don't really know what it's like at college, but they have all kinds of expectations. How much should you tell them? You have to tell them something but how much? Well, there are a lot of questions...and they come fast.

You can tell how fast things go because people often do two things at once. They study while they eat...or they grab a bite and run. Who has time for a regular old cooked meal? People are reading on the way over to class. They *cram* before exams; cramming is fast learning. There is a rush to get term papers and assignments done. There seems to be a rush to do everything but sleep.

Things are competitive too. No matter how many professors tell you that they don't grade on the curve, you know that one person's A is another person's E. Students are not encouraged to help each other much in college. There is a sort of unspoken competition in almost all programs. There's a lot of competition for friends and social groups too. You already know that. There is always pressure to be cool, to wear the right clothes, be seen with the right people, to use the right slang. Interestingly enough, being cool even extends to your choice of courses and your curriculum. Maybe everybody you know is taking business, you'd like to be with your friends, yet somehow you always had a hankering to write poetry. Maybe this year it's in to study engineering, but you just scraped by high school algebra.

Let's not forget the issue of money. Not so much making money after you graduate but making money enough to survive while you are here. Most students work while going to college these days in order to make ends meet. So where to find a job? How to get one that won't conflict with your class schedule. Maybe you're so tired getting home from work that you don't feel like studying. There is student money available, but how do you see about getting it?

I might close this description with a reminder of a process that sums up a lot of frustration in college, Drops and Adds. Adding a course to your schedule or dropping one is often a very tedious and frustrating process. I have sat in my university gymnasium at a table looking at long lines of desperate students, each one having to fit a course into a certain time slot. By the time it comes to Add time, everyone knows that most of the classes worth taking, most of the professors worth studying under, are long since taken. A lot of the time there is nothing available at all! Here you are at college and you can't even get a full schedule!

I am getting tired just listing the problems, and I know I have left a lot of them out. Is there a general direction a student can take in dealing with all of this? I think there is. If I had to use one key word in the whole business of surviving in college, that word would be EXPERIMENT.

By experimenting, I mean a willingness to try new and different things. What things? Mainly the things you are drawn to, things you have a hankering to do. This refers to courses and curricula; it refers to living; it refers to friends, to how you eat and drink. It even refers to the whole area of morality and religion. I don't mean that you have to try all the things you've had a hankering to do at once, but I do mean that I think the whole reason for going to college can be summed up by that one word, experiment. Your experimenting may not be at all dramatic to other people; it doesn't have to be. Most of our lives are made up of very small decisions. Your experiment may be no more earthshaking than telling off your roommate for borrowing your socks without asking, or raising your hand in class to ask a question, or telling your boyfriend to go to hell. Experimenting means having your eyes open for new things. It's like going to a clothing store and trying on everything in the place you think you might possibly like. Who is to say what will fit you until you try it on? That's what experimenting is.

Experimenting is like swinging a bat in a baseball game; you can't get a hit unless you swing at the ball. True, you may strike out a lot, but the hits only go to the people who take their cuts. A lot of this book will be about experimenting. A lot of this book will be about things you have never tried before.

This book will be most useful to those who try some of the

things it suggests. It isn't meant to be the kind of book you just read to pass the time; it isn't meant to be like watching a soap opera, where you just turn off the set when the half hour is over and walk away. Every chapter in this book is meant to be a challenge to experiment. Put another way, every chapter in this book is meant to help you find out what is special about you and what you can do with your own unique self. Experimenting and college are both about finding yourself. I don't know of a better reason to go to college than searching for your own best self; I don't know a way to find yourself other than the way of trying on different hats, the way of experimentation.

CHAPTER TWO

Finding Your Deep Self

We ended the last chapter saying that the rest of this book would be about experimenting. The first part of the chapter was about some of the confusing things you might have found on a college campus. I'm sure there are some confusing things in your life that are not in that chapter. I'm not asking you to leave those out of your considerations just because I didn't notice them. The point is, there are a lot of confusing things on a college campus. One of the first experiments I want to talk to you about is how to deal with the confusion.

I am going to presume that at other times in your life, before you got here, there were special places you went for peace and quiet. College is generally not a quiet time. I don't just mean blaring stereos in the dorms or loud people in the halls. There is another kind of noise that keeps you from being quiet inside. It is the noise of conflicting voices within yourself. Something in you says you want to go out; another voice within says to stay home; yet a third raises the question should you study or listen to music or call your girlfriend on the phone. There can be a lot of those voices making a terrible racket within you. It's a struggle, really, a tug of war; most important, such struggles are exhausting.

Where have you gone in the past when you needed to get away from it all? Let's make a list; I can tell you some of the places I have gone, but you must fill in your own. My places are only to suggest yours. When I was in my late teens, I used to put a sign on the door of my room saying, "Don't try to find me. I'm gone fishing." I'd borrow my Dad's rod and reel, grab a sleeping bag and a backpack. Then I'd walk the mile from our house to the highway and hitchhike thirty miles out to the country. There was a little stream I knew about called Fox Creek, running through the Ozark foothills outside my home town of St. Louis, Missouri. It was clear and cold; there were a few bass in it, and the farmer who owned the land was friendly. When I got there, I'd hide my sleeping bag and pack under a bush, stick a candy bar and a sandwich in my pocket, and fish until it got dark. There was a little cafe down the road called the Al-Pac; they'd cook a fish for you if you were lucky enough to catch one. I'd eat there by myself and then walk back to my sleeping bag. I'd lie on my back, comfortable and cozy and look at the stars. Then off to sleep; once in a while a freight train would rumble by on the nearby Missouri Pacific right of way, but I didn't mind the noise. In fact I loved the sound of the whistle all those old steam locomotives had. The whistle would begin very high and then trail off as the train moved down the track, a lonesome whistle that reminded me how cozy and warm I was in my sleeping bag. Once in a while it would rain on a trip like that, but the hot Missouri summer sun dried you out pretty fast. A couple of days fishing in Fox Creek would just heal me, making me feel nice and brown and sunburned and all in one piece, ready to go back home and face the world again.

Fox Creek was a good place for me. It wasn't a luxury, it was a necessity. All my good voices came back to me out there; most of the discordant ones left. I did not spend the time trying to figure my life out; I spent the time fishing. In retrospect, I can see that it is better to use places like Fox Creek not as places at which to figure out the problems in one's life. Rather, such places are spots of peace where one puts cares and troubles on the back burner to simmer. A lot of confusion unravels itself if we have a place to go that has nothing to do with the confusion. I have named you one of mine from long ago when I was in my late teens.

There are a lot of other places I use today for shorter times. My garden is a good one, provided there is no basketball game going on outside the garage of my neighbors. Escaping to the bathroom is surely part of the escape mechanisms of countless Americans. Closing the door of your own room works for some people. There is a big field a mile from my house today where I sometimes go by myself to pick raspberries or wild strawberries. Once in a while I walk on a golf course at night looking for night crawlers. All these places have one thing in common. For me, they are peaceful; they bring rest to my soul. Somehow the quiet that is in each one of them helps me quiet down inside. It happens very slowly, usually without my noticing it.

At this point I want you to list all your quiet places. They don't have to be places you still go to. Just recall them and write them down. Just remembering them can be a peaceful exercise. Above all, remembering them will remind you how important those places are. If you haven't found any of them here at college, your list will remind you to start looking.

Any treatment of peaceful places involves what you do at those places. Peaceful places beget peaceful activities. Fox Creek was a peaceful place where I spent a lot of time doing a peaceful activity, fishing. But it may help you to think of the activities themselves, for they are not always tied to certain places.

I remember once sitting with a friend of mine on top of a hill overlooking the Missouri River. It was a hot August evening out in the country. We each carried a wine bottle full of homemade root beer, still cold from the cooler. As it grew dark we sat on that hill and looked over the valley. We could see the lights on a train far below in the river valley. The shadows were warm and friendly; the root beer cold and sweet. I felt very close to my friend there as we talked softly in the dark. We talked casually and easily not wondering what we were going to say next. We talked about our families and how beautiful the light was, as it faded slowly on the western horizon, about the lights on the freight train below, about the river which shone like a great black snake in the valley. And when we went back home, we slept well and peacefully.

So, watching a sunset with a friend can be a peaceful activity. Sometimes writing letters to friends does it for me, or taking a walk in the woods, riding a motorcycle or driving a car. I have a friend who likes to play golf early in the morning with no shoes on, early enough so that nobody else is there and he doesn't have to pay.

What are your quiet sports and pastimes? I know that I myself have only scratched the surface. There is the whole world of music and the arts. There is curling up with a good book or a favorite program when no one is in the house. There's fishing and hunting and backpacking. Make a list of your own peace giving activities. They are no more luxuries than going to peaceful places is. You need them.

I have talked about looking out over a valley with a friend on a hot August evening, which brings up favorite times and seasons. Everyone has favorite times, even if they've never formally thought about it. I have always loved spring, for example. It reminds me that winter doesn't last forever. For years now I have written an old student of mine every Spring because we both get very worn down in the winter. Often we are discouraged at the end of all the cold and dark that come with the winter months in Michigan. For both of us spring is a miracle, just seeing trees coming back to life, crocuses coming up, water melting. I like to get out into the streets in front of my house when the snow starts to melt and dig out the drain in the curb where it has lain covered with snow all winter. Then I watch the stream of water from the melting ice run into the iron grill of the drain. I make channels along the edge of the street, get soaking wet myself, and can lose a whole afternoon out there in front of my house being a part of it all. For I know that spring means Easter and new life, a sort of annual resurrection of all nature that has been cooped up and cramped and lifeless during the Winter.

There are important times of day too. I like it very late at night, maybe at the tail end of a party. Most of the guests are gone; only a few very strong ones left. The music and drinking part of the evening are over and it is quiet. One night, or I should say early morning, years ago, I remember taking a walk in the snow with my cousin Jane, who was sixteen, to my forty years of age. It must have been about five o'clock, the sun just starting to come up as we trudged down the middle of the street; there was no traffic and no noise. Jane told me how beautiful she thought people were, we were both in awe of the rising sun and the quiet, a little bit in love with each other, but not in a bad sense. We felt close to each other and we talked quietly of beauty and of God. It was a special time.

I like to go backpacking during Spring Break. It's the first week in March each year. A colleague of mine and I throw our packs and some supplies into my VW van and head for Tennessee and the Smoky Mountains. Each year we go, we nearly freeze; it's still cold up high in the mountains even as far south as Tennessee, but there is a joy of those long days, pitting yourself against the mountain slopes, in long periods of walking with little or no talking. As if in the hard work of carrying a pack on the trail somehow all the stored up devils of Winter get squeezed out of your system. That freeze-dried food tastes like something out of a five star French restaurant. Sleeping in our tiny packer's tent, sometimes on snow, is like the sleep of a child. It's usually twelve hours before either of us wakes up. Spring time in the Smokies is a special time for me.

Now, what are your special times of year? Write them down; get them to come back to you. What are your special times of day? Write those down too, remember the best ones in detail. Here at school it is possible to forget those times; it is possible to ignore or overlook them, so that they are robbed of their power to restore you, to let the deepest part of yourself grow and stretch, so that you have the strength to handle the rat race.

And so, we have talked about quiet times, quiet places, and quiet activities—all with the idea of letting the surface noise die down and letting one's deepest voices speak. There is another activity I'd like to talk to you about; it isn't a sport; it can be done at any time of day or night and almost anywhere that has enough light and space for a person to be able to write. I'm talking about keeping a journal. By a journal I don't mean just a record of activities or how much it has rained in the month of June in Kalamazoo or Oshkosh. I mean a record of your personal thoughts and feelings. They are related to what you do; if you are like me, they are related to whether it rained or not in the month of June in Kalamazoo, because rain keeps me inside and bothers my allergies. All these have a lot to do with what I think and feel.

Speaking of feelings, I believe it is a good idea to write down your bad feelings as well as your good ones. Bad feelings are like bullies; if you face a bully, a lot of the time he (or she) will back down and leave you alone. If you write down your bad feelings, a lot of the time they are robbed of their power to take away your peace of mind. It is as if by writing them down you call them by name; when you know someone's name you have a lot of power over them.

I recall my first year of teaching. It was in a boy's high school in Kansas City, Missouri. In the beginning I didn't know the names of any of the kids there. When school was over in the afternoon, I was supposed to stay for a few minutes down in the school basement where the boys had their lockers. Those kids jived me fifty different ways. They'd come up to me and ask me really stupid questions with elaborate seriousness. "Sir, do you know where the principal's office is?" or "Sir, I think there's a boa constrictor in my locker." "Mr. Gross, somebody took all my books." It was all a put on designed to embarrass a green teacher. Little by little, I got to know the names of those kids, and the put ons mysteriously disappeared. I'd say, "Well, Pete, I guess you have to buy some new books," or "I'm not surprised there's a snake in your locker, Kevin." Knowing somebody's name changes things.

Writing down hard times and feelings of hurt or sadness gets those unruly dragons down on a piece of paper where you can see them and know them. It cuts them down to size. Bad feelings are like the monsters you used to worry about under your bed when you were a kid. They grow and grow if you are afraid to look under the bed to see just how big they actually are.

Good feelings and good ideas are surely worth while writing down, too. If you write them down, you are far more likely to remember them; they are a source of strength. You can go back and reexperience them by reading the back pages of your journal.

Keeping a journal is a way of tuning into your deep self. It is a way of underlining what is best in you and keeping the things that bother you from gettng out of hand. I don't have any rule on how often to write in a journal. That depends on you. There will be times when you want to write every day; there are other times, especially the busy ones, when you just don't think about it.

One of the things you'll notice after you have kept a journal for a year or two; there will be themes that keep coming back. Maybe you write down that you noticed a certain guy in line in your dorm cafeteria. Maybe you never write about him again. On the other hand, his name may keep cropping up. You'll want to pay attention to that. Or, one night there was a group talking about going to Europe or how interesting it is to play the electric guitar. You listen; you are interested, and you write the experience down in your diary. How interesting it would be if a year from now, you still want to go to Europe or you still find yourself looking at electric guitars in store windows. The thoughts and desires that keep coming up in your journal are always important. Generally speaking, it's my opinion that wishes which keep coming back are the ones you should pay most attention to. A journal helps you to know which are the important desires and which are the ones that seem important only for a day.

A note on how to write. You are writing for yourself, not anybody else. You don't need me to tell you that you can write naturally; there's no need for putting on or showing off; you can just be yourself. That's a plus right there. A lot of people write down things they think they should have done. They scribble away about missed opportunities. They fill pages with what they ought to do. Sometimes that takes the joy and power out of keeping a journal. It becomes a dreary list of missed opportunities and wrong turns. I would suggest making a deal with yourself not to write down the words "should have" or "ought" in your journal.

If you want to, write about something that didn't turn out right. Describe it as it happened. If you want to change your way of handling such things, then write down what you plan to change. But don't torture yourself with what might have been or what you ought to have done. That's like picking at old sores; they don't heal when you pick at them. Writing up "shoulds" and "oughts" won't change you; it will just make you feel bad. You change by deciding on a new course of action not by worrying about old mistakes.

Another very fruitful area for keeping a journal is the whole world of dreams. It is a commonplace that we all dream and that dreams have a lot to do with what is going on in our lives under the surface. If you want to get to know yourself, get to know your dreams. Journal keeping helps you remember them. I find dreams often let me know if something is bothering me that I don't want to admit to my conscious self. Sometimes I have marvelous, reassuring dreams that remind me of all the good things I have going for myself. It's good to write the good ones down; they will remind you of hidden strengths you have that you might forget about.

If you have a tendency to forget your dreams, try writing in your journal right when you get up in the morning. If you wake up at night, keep your journal by your bedside, so that you can write in it the very moment you wake up.

Whole libraries have been written about the meaning of dreams and how to interpret them. I myself think that with a little practice it is not so hard as some of the learned psychologists would have us think. I have mentioned before that everybody knows good dreams from bad dreams, kids and grownups alike. As for the further content, I have found it helpful to know that almost everyone and everything in my dreams can be legitimately seen as an aspect of myself.

I had a dream some years ago that may show you what I mean. I dreamt I was walking barefooted along a beach of rough sand. There was a stream of water, deep and fast-moving between me and an island across the stream from me, a stream of perhaps fifty feet in width. It came to me as I walked the sandy shore that I could swim across the channel, despite the current, despite the channel, the depth, and the coldness of the water. It would be a risky business, but I was up to it. I had a feeling of joy and exhileration as I stood poised at the edge of the channel, just before I dived in to swim across to the other side.

I had the dream at a time in my life when I was having a hard time in my post as a university professor. I had left a secure position in my home town, gone to graduate school in a foreign country, and was now teaching in a completely new place, often feeling a fish out of water. The dream reminded me that I had taken plunges many times in my life and survived them all. This present crisis was the way my life had often been; the dream was a reminder to me that I was equal to the task and that if I would let the excitement of it seep into my bones instead of worrying about it, this new task in a new place could be interesting. The fact that I wrote the dream down fixed it in my mind, instead of letting the image slip away.

There are, to be sure, dreams whose meaning you will have trouble getting to the bottom of. Sometimes a dream won't come clear to you for a long time, but they are important to self understanding. Poets, song writers, and ordinary people have taken dreams seriously for as far back as we have recorded history, without the benefit of special training. You can too. If you are so inclined, and your dreams remain interesting to you, you are, after all at a university. Somewhere in your university's offerings there will be a course on the interpretation of dreams.

Quiet places, quiet activities, quiet times, keeping a journal of your ideas, feelings, and dreams. All of these are ordinary means for getting in touch with what is deepest in you; they are means for getting to know yourself better; they are means for keeping your cool during any time of stress; they are valuable tools for dealing with college life.

Lest you get the idea that this book is going to be only about reaching inside yourself, let's get ready at this point to shift to another aspect of college life, the basics of study. College is about studying books as well as getting to know yourself. Every semester has courses, classrooms, papers, and reading. They are vital to a good experience on campus. Tackling the basic rules of study is our next subject.

CHAPTER THREE

The Bare Bones of Study

The barest essentials of good study habits are two: having a place to study and having a regular time to work. Getting to be a good student is a matter of rhythm, getting into the swing of your courses, so that days and weeks and months go by with regular progress in learning. You can't learn it all in giant gulps. Learning takes place slowly, the way water drips off a rock in a cave. A steady drip is the key. In order to get this steadiness you need a place that you can rely on to be quiet day after day, week after week, month after month. Once in a while, your room will be that place, but the trouble with your room is that other people know how to find you there, people who are not as concerned with your doing well in school as you are.

Where to find such a place? I can only hint. You have to do the finding. One good place to check out is the college or university library. Some libraries have smaller branches, a business library, say, or a library for fine arts. The branch libraries might be more convenient for you as you look for a quiet place to study. Colleges and universities have all sorts of nooks and crannies. You have to nose around. You'd be surprised how many little alcoves there are. The college newspaper or literary magazine will have an office, dorms sometimes have special study rooms. There are classrooms that don't get used much. I often correct papers after class right in my classroom if there's no class following mine. I remember discovering that my college newspaper had a small office that wasn't used by anybody at night; a friendly editor lent me a key. I studied there for a whole semester, before the editor graduated and a less friendly new one would no longer let me study there. Then I had to look for a new place. The point is, somewhere there is a quiet place; you must be willing to keep an eye out for such a place. Without a quiet place, you won't be a good student.

Besides a regular place you need a regular time. You can't just study any old time, or once in a while, or just before exams. Remember you need a rhythm that goes from week to week if you are going to learn. It's a matter of setting yourself a schedule and sticking to it. Writing it down is a good idea; that will help to keep you honest. Put that schedule right in your journal and check once in a while to see that you are keeping to it. Usually a schedule will have to be revised after an initial period. There will be other things that come up which you haven't thought about when you first sat down at the beginning of a new semester to make your study schedule.

What might such a schedule look like? I think it's a bad idea to make a very complicated one, with different times for study each day. Those are hard to keep; you'll probably get mixed up as to which day is which and lose your regular rhythm. You don't want to assign yourself so many hours of study that deep down you know you won't keep to what you have decided either. A reasonable amount of time five days a week and one of the weekend days. Here's a sample: Monday through Thursday 8:00-10:00 P.M., Friday 4:00-6:00. Saturday 4:00-6:00 P.M. That may not seem like a lot to you but you will be amazed how much you will learn in a semester if you stick to a schedule like that. If you are going to be gone on a Saturday, then make up the hours on Sunday or another day, but don't make too many exceptions. Regularity is the thing. You will gradually discover your best times for study as you go from semester to semester. Having a schedule will become almost automatic. In the beginning, however, you'll have to work hard at sticking to it. You may even have to have the experience of finding yourself on academic probation before you realize how necessary a schedule is.

So, a place to study and a regular time. What else is there to the bare bones of study? I am going to presume that you realize you must go to class. That's even more basic than your study schedule. Most profs will have some basic rules about absence; it's a good thing to notice those. Generally they reduce to your being allowed to miss three classes in a three hour course per semester. I'm not going to labor the point.

My point here has to do with what you do while you are in class. When you are in class you take notes. There are almost no exceptions. You learn to take down the basic ideas that the professor is putting out. You've already discovered that you can't get every word; there are too many words to get them all. The idea is to make an outline. An outline is a skeleton in written form. It consists of the major topics of a given class. Let's see if I can give you an example.

Let us suppose that your professor comes into class and says that he is going to discuss the first four stages in human life as understood by Erik Erikson. Right away you have the title for your notes:

Erikson's 1st 4 Stages

You will notice that I don't spell out either the word "first" or the word "four." When you are taking notes, you will gradually develop ways of writing things more quickly; shortening words is one way to do that. It saves both time and space on the page you're writing on. Your notes are basically for you. You don't turn them in for the professor ordinarily. Other students don't have to be able to read them either. So, you can take some short cuts.

Back to our lecture on Erikson. After giving you the title of the matter for the hour of class, the professor begins with stage one. He calls this the stage of the newborn child. It is a time characterized by a struggle within the baby between two qualities: trust and mistrust. Most of the next fifteen minutes is taken describing this stage. Your notes?

I. Stage One: trust vs. mistrust
   A. Trust. Directly to do with the mothering figure. Mother most important. Tied to being held, nursing, being rocked, sung to. Very physical between mother and baby. Lasts about a year.
   B. Mistrust. Mom can't hold baby all the time. Baby is hungry, wants to be held, gets wet or has poopy pants. Gets mad, feels betrayed when mother isn't there.
   C. Trust AND Mistrust. Kids learn both at same time. We hope trust predominates, but mistrust important for life too. A struggle between the two.

These might be the notes for fifteen or twenty minutes of class time. They are carefully placed under headings. The main heading is indicated by a Roman numeral. In this case Roman numeral I. Under this heading are upper case letters of the alphabet, A., B., C., and so forth. You will note that I have indicated the letters of the alphabet more than Roman numeral I. As soon as the professor goes on to another heading the note taker will switch with the professor. So when the prof announces that she will now move from one to Erikson's stage two, the student moves with her.....

   II.   Stage Two: Autonomy vs. Shame and Doubt

Back to the upper class letters of the alphabet for subheadings.

     A. Autonomy. Means independence, pride, standing up. Age: around two. Fits with baby learning to stand. Very willful. Terrible twos. Hard to handle. Problem for parents.

     B. Shame. Parents have to do it! Has to do with exposure. Caught with pants down. Caught in the act. Being seen when you don't want to be...that's being shamed. Connection with toilet training. Necessary but bad to overdo. Child can lose sense of herself if too much shaming.

     C. Doubt. Too much shaming can lead to kid's doubting his good points. Hesitation and doubt, second guessing. Being self-conscious in later life.

     D. Autonomy vs. shame and doubt. A mixture of these for good development. Independence good...but kids have to learn to respect others...shaming.

Now, I wouldn't expect you to be able to follow these notes perfectly, because they are MY notes. They are much neater than classnotes generally are too.

It is a good idea to go over your notes after class and to write them up more neatly, when they are still fresh in your mind. Nothing is more useless than your own notes if they are so messy and brief that even you can't make sense out of them when time to review comes. By the way, one of the things that happens when you go back over your notes to rewrite them is that your understanding of the matter will become more thorough. The things you still don't understand will be more obvious. The stuff you must memorize will start to become fixed in your memory.

You will develop all sorts of things of your own that are not in my model notes, things that are peculiar to you. Some students use different color pencils for different things. As I noted earlier, each student will develop a sort of familiar short-hand of her own; you will have your own abbreviations and ways of reminding yourself of important points in a class. Still, they must be compressed. They must be orderly. Above all, they must be clear enough so that when it comes time to review, you'll be able to understand them.

At this point I'd like to add that becoming a good note taker takes time. You won't learn it overnight. In the beginning your notes may be so short that you can't figure out what they mean. They may be so long that it takes forever to rewrite them. You may frequently miss the important points in a given class. One thing is sure, even poor notes are better than relying on your memory alone during class time. Taking notes will help you pay attention too.

So far, everything I have said about taking class notes takes it for granted that your professor is an orderly presenter of material. Some profs almost defy their students to take notes. Their lectures may ramble all over the place without much order. Or the whole class may be run on a discussion basis instead of a nice, neat lecture. Discussions, you will find, although often more interesting than lectures, are much harder to get down in your notes. It may be impossible to get nice neat headings and subheadings. You will have to have an alternate way of taking notes in such classes. I don't think it is a good idea not to take any notes just because your professor gets off the point or runs her class using a discussion format.

In more loosely organized classes, see if you can get hold of a general topic or a general question. Write down the topic or question. Then get as much as you can down which seems to fit the question. When the discussion or lecture veers off in another direction, try to think of another heading or question, write it down, and put as much as you can down under this heading until the topic changes yet again. You may not want to bother with Roman numerals and large case letters of the alphabet . . . the class is just too jumbled for that.

Let's see if I can give you an example. Suppose there is a

discussion about the meaning of Erikson's first stage: Trust vs. Mistrust. Students are firing questions at the prof from all angles. Your notes might look like this:

Q. Isn't trust an issue all the way through life?

A. Yes, that's true. Special importance to the first year of life. Foundation for later trust. Babies neglected by moms have trouble trusting later. Trust a sort of foundation for later life. Can be learned later, but it's harder.

Q. Suppose the mother dies?

A. For kid to have normal life, someone else must do mothering—nurses, another mother, Dad?, SOMEBODY must hold it, feed it, rock it. Special question of premature babies in incubators.

Q. Seems like your life could be wrecked for good in its very first year.

A. A really bad first year will make the rest of life harder; true. People do overcome these things. Babies are sometimes abused, beaten, starved, and spoiled. Makes it hard to trust later. All of us have stages that have not turned out well. These have a way of being the negative side of our characters.

Q. Does this mean that we don't have any freedom? Are we programmed to be mistrusting or trusting early on?

A. Yes and no. Early formation does last...we also have the freedom to fight our dark sides, to renegotiate stages, that were bad ones in our childhoods. It is almost always better to learn trust as a baby than to have to start almost from scratch later.

This format in note taking allows for more wandering class presentation. The "Q" stands for question. The "A" stands for Answer.

The fact is, "One size fits all" doesn't work for class notes. You adapt to the situation, but you almost always will do better in your course if you can learn to take down something legible in each class period. I am a believer myself in having a separate spot in my notes for each class. Trying to put all of your classes into one notebook runs the risk of getting all the notes so jumbled that you can never get them in order. Some sort of order is necessary. The bottom line, of course, is how well you do in a given course. If you are doing just fine, don't change your system of notetaking.

If we have been talking about taking notes in class, there is a close parallel between classroom note taking and note taking for assigned readings. Again, you must use discernment; you must size up a reading assignment in deciding what kind of notes to take. If there is a novel assigned, the most important thing may be to finish the novel. If you spend too much time taking notes, you may never finish the book. Even in such lengthy assignments as novels, I'd recommend some kind of notes, even if it's only writing down the meaning of the title of the book and the names and correct spellings of the chief characters. Perhaps a very short paragraph on the plot of the story...or a couple of comments on what you liked or disliked in the book. Classroom discussion or lecture that follows the reading of a book can provide you with good notes on the book, provided, of course, that you have read the book.

The way this chapter has gone so far, it seems that if you learn good note taking techniques for both classroom and home reading, you'll have it made in college. As if order were the key to everything. Thank God, it isn't. Being orderly can really help you but it isn't everything. There is something else in the life of study that is a lot more important than order. That something is interest.

I really don't think that you or I, or anybody else can continue to study, week after week, without being interested in the stuff to be studied. You may be able to fake it for a while. You may be able to work a semester or two to please your parents or your own sense of duty, but your work will suffer sooner or later if you continue to take courses that bore you.

There is a strange American dream that infects us all to some extent, it is the dream that we will be living the good life if and when we get rich. This dream affects college students in a very destructive way sometimes. If you decide to take courses in engineering or business or fashion design solely because you have it on good authority that a degree in one of these fields will cause you to make a lot of money when you graduate, you are a fool. Well, perhaps you are not a fool, but you will have been fooled. Someone will have pulled the wool over your eyes. You will have been sold a bill of goods.

Why do I say that? Simply because I know that there must be an inner attraction for a given course of study to do well in it. Most people find this out the hard way. Poor grades and boredom in college go right together. Your task as a beginning college student is to find courses and a curriculum that are interesting to you. That's where experimenting comes in; you may be one of the lucky few who already know what they are drawn to. Most of us have to find out by trial and error which courses interest us the most.

The sane approach to college directs that out of one's interesting courses, one finds an interesting major area of study. There is a lot of thrashing around involved in this process; it is painful and hard. Still, it is nowhere near so painful and hard as taking courses merely because someone told you that's where the money is.

Look at it this way. Even if you managed to get yourself trained to be really good at something that paid very well and at the same time you hated every second you spent at this skill, what would you have? You'd be miserable all week at the work place and then have to make up for a miserable week by spending your money on the weekends and vacations. You don't have to be a Math major to figure out how much of your life would be satisfying if you were to live your life for the times you are free from your work.

I realize, and you probably do too, that no course of study is going to guarantee you a happy work life. Life isn't that simple. Still, if you find an area of study that is genuinely interesting, you will have gotten a start at least for leading an interesting life later. Job opportunities are far more likely to be interesting if you train yourself in something you find challenging and enjoyable, than if you just drudge your way through a course of studies you hope will make up in money for what it lacks in fun. Don't forget that poor grades even in a program that yields high paying jobs will not help you get the job. Poor grades and boredom are sisters.

While you are scratching around for interesting courses, I might say a word about instructors. Make a point of finding out who the good teachers are. It pays off; sometimes I think interesting classes are much more who the teacher is than what the class matter is. A really interesting teacher will open up potential interests which you were never aware of. How do you find out who the good ones are? I think you know this better than I do. You ask, ask, ask. Ask students, ask teachers, ask anybody. The word does get out who the good instructors are. If you are nosy enough, you can find out.

A basic approach to getting a line on what you want to do

with yourself in college is to take your general education requirements first. They will give you a broad look at a number of different fields of study. You can find out by trying which ones you like. Your university will demand that you take some variety of courses to fulfill your general education requirements anyway. You can be getting requirements out of the way and at the same time exploring for your major. Don't pass out if you don't find an interesting area right away. I would suggest that you don't decide too quickly what curriculum you want. It's worthwhile fishing for a while before you decide. Put another way, you may think you know exactly what you want when you arrive at school. A semester later you may no longer know. I remember a fine student who began college studying art, and wound up in social work. I have a niece who began in art and is finishing in business. There's nothing strange about either one of them. They just had to experiment, to try new things before making a commitment. For some people the hardest thing is narrowing things down; they are interested in a lot of things. Others discover that there are only a few things in college that interest them, and it's hard hanging on long enough to find out what those things are. And, of course, there are always some for whom a couple of years of college is a sort of interlude in which they find that college life itself is something they do not want to live. Maybe later but not now. That in itself is a discovery, a challenge; I do not think anyone should regard it as a defeat if he or she decides that now is not the time for college. There are lots of reasons for not going to college, good reasons too. This book is not about surviving outside of college, however, but surviving inside, so I'll have to let those who don't want to be here after giving a good, hard look, be on their way.

Is there more to college than being organized and finding interesting courses? Yes, but I don't think that there is anything more important, as far as the life of study goes. There is the small matter of what you might call classroom manners. We'll be getting on to that in the next chapter.

CHAPTER FOUR

Classroom Politics and Manners

A college classroom is like a home. There are some basic rules that you'd be well to follow if you want to get along here. Those rules are not all that different from the basics of getting along with high school teachers. There are some differences, though.

You can save yourself a lot of trouble if you know the basic rules of politeness in a college classroom. Few colleges and universities have bells to tell you when you are on time or late. When it gets to be time, class starts. Some profs come early, some come late, but almost none of them appreciate students who come in after class begins. If you have to leave early, it is basic politeness to tell your professor that you have to go at such and such a time; that way she knows you're not stalking out in a huff. As far as being on time goes, there is the advantage of being able to choose your own seat. Very few classes have assigned seats. The rule is usually first come, first served. If you want the least desirable seat in the room, keep coming late. Coming late also draws attention to yourself on the part of the prof in a way that you want it the least.

It is good to know as well that your professors will get to know you very slowly. Frequently you have a given prof for only one semester. The whole atmosphere is different from high school for that reason. Back in high school, most classes go for a full school year. Your teachers got to know you there. Here it is often not like that. If you are not there, you're not there. No fuss is made, generally, until grade time. If you miss a lot of class, there is often no warning by your teacher until it is too late. It's good to know that.

What do you call your profs? You can't go wrong with professor, but that's very formal. Just keep your ears open, you'll get a hint. If you are in doubt, ask. Who cares? Remember, I call this chapter the politics of the classroom. Politicians learn to get along with their constituents or they don't get reelected. Students are smart to learn to get along with their profs. I do think professors are generally fair and impartial with students, but it will never do you any harm to treat them right. I'm not talking about what high school students call being a brown nose. I'm talking about getting along, and incidentally not making a fool of yourself in front of your fellow students.

Once in a while I get a college student or two who thinks he is still in high school. One of the old high school games, of course, is trying to get the teacher's goat. Loud talking, purposely stupid questions—things like that. Those games are not hard for a college professor to handle because inevitably the students who pull that kind of stuff really look silly. Other students generally freeze them out.

So much for getting along. Manners are really the easy part. Just call your prof the name he or she seems at ease with and come on time. Know the absence rules and keep them. Let the prof know if you have to leave early.

There is another more basic aspect to getting along in class and that is figuring out what your professor wants. That's one place where class notes are so useful because most college professors lecture on their favorite ideas; most of them give exams on their favorite ideas too. If you take good notes, you have the basis for a good review for tests. It is good classroom politics to find out what your instructor's favorite ideas are and then to learn them.

I am not advocating becoming a door mat or a hypocrite. Think your own thoughts; be your own person. Just because you tell the professor what he wants to hear doesn't mean you are trading in your own values or your own ability to make up your own mind. Nobody can tell you what to think. Telling a prof what she wants to hear doesn't mean you have been brainwashed. It doesn't mean you are insincere either. Let's put it another way. Size up your professor. If he or she is the kind of person who invites disagreement, disagree all you want, giving your reasons, of course. If, however, your instructor is limited and feels insecure when students disagree, you should notice that. One thing is pretty sure, the grade you get is made up by your professor; profs have a lot of power here and of course, you have to live with the grade. Keep that in mind before you decide to raise too much hell in class.

If you do want to disagree, sometimes it is much better to do so in the privacy of your professor's office where he won't feel so much on the spot.

You'll never do yourself any harm by asking a professor for help. You may get one or two who won't help you but it doesn't hurt to ask.

So much for professors. They're just people; they appreciate politeness like other people; like most people, they'll help you if you ask them. Like most people they have favorite ideas. There are other sources of good ideas in the classroom too. I'm referring to students. You may not know any of them at the start of class; big schools are like that, but you can get to know a few of them if you want to. If you do, you may have a friend at the end of the semester to review with. If you missed a class or just didn't understand something, there's a chance one of your classmates knows what you don't know. Students can work together; there's no law against it. Keep an eye out for the smart ones you might be able to get along with. You can probably help each other. Students learn more from each other in the college years than they do from their professors; there's no doubt about that in my mind. Having a buddy to talk ideas with is a great gift. Having a buddy to talk ideas with that directly concern an examination can help your grade besides contributing to your interest. And interest, you will recall, is the most important thing in surviving in college.

We've skirted the notion of examinations in this chapter as well as in the chapter on the bare bones of study. Tests and exams are important; there's no getting out of them. That leads us to the topic of the next chapter.

CHAPTER FIVE

Taking Examinations

Taking exams takes the whole college experience and puts it in a nutshell. If everything else is going well, your exams will go well. In terms of how this book is written, if you are beginning to get a line on your school, that helps at exam time. If you have managed to find quiet places and times, that will help too. If you have figured out a place to study and a time to study, the payoff is at exam time. If you have observed the basic politics of the classroom, you'll have made a pretty good guess as to what your prof is going to ask and you won't have needlessly brought the focus of her attention to yourself by coming late or acting as though you were in high school in the classroom. You will have ferreted out a student or two in class to review with too. You will be all set for those horrible things called exams.

Most of your preparation for an examination must be done alone, just as most of your study must be done alone. The word "review" is a good one here because it means "viewing again" or "taking a second look." What you hope for as a student is to have no new matter to look at. Your task is to get the old matter down. At the risk of being nauseatingly repetitive, this is where good notes come into play. You don't want to spend much time on your textbooks. You have boiled them down in your notes; you have filled in around these notes with the notes you have taken in class. Your task is to reduce these notes to something you can learn. One of the characteristics of a good review is the making of your notes even smaller. Making notes of your notes is another way of putting it. You may want to clarify from time to time by looking something up in a book, but for the most part a good review is done from good notes. Going through the books takes too much time.

There will almost always be some matter you must know word for word: formulas, dates, definitions. Memory work

31

takes place automatically as you take notes; when you try to boil your notes down your memory is at work still. There are final steps, just looking at the fairly small amount of stuff you must commit to memory; testing yourself, reciting it to your roommate or classmate. Brute memory work is best done in small time periods, not more than a half hour over a period of days. You'll just go blank if you try to spend too long at it.

When you are going over your notes or your digest of your notes, it's not a bad idea to use a highlighter or a colored ball point pen to indicate which parts of your notes you know best and which ones need work. Check them off. One of the things I do when I really get sick of studying my notes is either to work on them with somebody else or to write comments on my own notes— almost anything that comes to mind. I call these notes "silly notes."

"For example, if I were trying to get my notes on Erikson's stage one down, if I had gotten so sick of looking at them that I could barely stand it, THEN I might write something like this:

Trust—rhymes with bust, rust, must, gust. What's great about trusting people? It will get you nothing but trouble. Here's a list of people who have hurt me when I trusted them: Mr. Korth, who slapped me in the face in the student cafeteria in high school, an old priest who embarrassed me to tears in Greek class in college, a policeman in New England who put me in jail once when I asked him for a place to spend the night, my "friends" who didn't elect me to any of the offices in my high school fraternity, Jane Curran, who stood me up on a date in high school...and lots of others!
Mistrust—Miss Trust? Miss who? I wouldn't miss trust at all. Who the hell is Miss Trust? Ms. Trust? My father told me never to trust a woman.
In the first year of life. I can't remember anything about my first year...zilch. How about having seen others? Both of my boys I saw a lot of when they were newborns. One was a screamer; the other was nice. The screamer got more attention. Do you suppose he's more trusting than his brother?

What's the idea behind writing a sort of stream of conscious about your notes? It does keep you in the general area yet one more time. Sometimes what you really think is never in your notes. Last but not least, it can loosen you up during your review.

I knew an old priest who taught high school who used to require all of his students to make crib notes before exams. He used to say that making crib notes was a great way to review the matter because you had to get everything you'd need on a small piece of paper that would be easy to conceal during the test. He said that most of the kids would know the matter well by the time they had taken so much trouble as to reduce it all to that tiny piece of paper, so why not let them use it openly?

There's a lot to that. And it brings up a whole matter of cheating during exams. I am reluctant to get too righteous about cheating, because I am aware that almost all students, including myself, have cheated at one time or another. A knowledgeable and experienced professor will give you an exam such that cheating will be very difficult. An open book exam is an example of such an exam. Or an essay exam: one or two long essays for the whole one or two hour period. It's hard to copy somebody else's essay.

How about a professor who is so slack as to make cheating very easy? Once in a while you get one of those. How about a prof who gives such hard examinations that you honestly think you couldn't pass without cheating? There are some of those too. Can you say that it is *always* wrong to cheat?

I think it is good to take a look at what cheating is. Generally speaking, cheating is petty theft. Most of the time what you are taking will not make you or break you as a student. There is a theft and a deception, that's true. You are saying that you know something that you don't know; that is a lie. The better grade that you will get, if you are a skillful cheater is not something that is really yours. That's stealing.

It is worth while pointing out that massive fraud is still rare in college, a kind of cheating that would dramatically change your grade point for the better. So, most cheating is not in the same category with robbing a bank or ruining someone else's good name or murder or rape. Most cheating is petty and not a big deal.

It is worth noting too, that there are surely times when cheating is justified. It is possible for a professor to ask for an impossible amount of work. It is possible to give an examination that has nothing to do with what everyone in the class was led to expect. In both the above cases, I think cheating would be justified. I also think that such cases don't come up very frequently.

The issue of cheating then reduces itself to whether or not you want to call yourself a petty thief and a person who tells small lies for his own convenience. There are times when any sane person would cheat without risk of being a liar or a thief. You have to take each case separately. I am all for honesty myself; I try to remember that I have cheated on occasion myself, even though I am not proud of it. I think it would be foolish for a student to expect mercy from a professor, should a student be caught in the act of cheating. Generally speaking, cheating is not only risky, it's dumb.

You'd be a lot smarter to spend the time you waste trying to see what's on someone else's paper looking carefully at the direction for the particular examination you are taking. I wish I had a nickel for every student who rushed through the exam instructions, being afraid of wasting time, and then put down a series of answers that the instructions simply didn't call for. It is important to give the instructions a good careful read. If there's something you don't understand, ask! When you have finished reading those instructions, read them again!

The small stuff. There's an old saying that advises, "Don't sweat the small stuff." That doesn't apply at examination time. The small stuff can be very important. Why? Because exam time is usually a tense time. It's more possible to panic when the heat is on. That, all by itself, is a good reason to pay attention to the small stuff surrounding examinations. The small things don't demand that you be a genius, or even that you have made a good review. Anybody can do the small things. What are they?

Coming early to the exam is one of them; that way if you get lost on the way or forget something, there's time to remedy the situation. That way you know you'll get a good chair; that way you'll get a few extra minutes to write if your instructor starts early. Above all, if you are early you won't have the terrible embarrassment of walking in late for an exam. If you come in late, you can get rattled and mess up a perfectly respectable review.

Another item considered small is bringing what you need, with extra supplies in case your pen runs out or you break your pencil. What is worse during an exam than to have your only ball point pen suddenly quit on you? You look wildly around the room for someone who might lend you one. You say every cuss word you know under your breath. You tell yourself that this can't be happening to you; it's a brand new pen; it CAN'T be quitting on you. What I am describing is called needless panic. When you finally get another pen from a reluctant friend or an exasperated professor, you may find that your train of thought has been so interrupted that you can't remember what you are writing. How much better to be one of the smug ones who bring a whole bag of ball points to exams. How much better to be one of those who remembers to bring a dictionary or calculator or exam notebook. It pays off to take the time to remember those little things when you are dealing with a tense situation to begin with.

If it is time to close this chapter on examinations and tests, I'll close it with a comment on time. Tests and exams are often situations where time is of the essence. You need to use every minute and you want every minute you can get. Wear a watch! You can use it to see how you are coming. If you lose track of time, you may be only halfway through when the time for the exam runs out. It helps to keep an eye on the amount of time you have and the amount of test you have to finish. Your professor can't guess what you really know if you leave a portion of a test unfinished. Another way of handling time is being willing to fight for a bit more time at the end of an exam. A lot of instructors can be leaned on a little if a student makes it clear that she needs a bit more time. Never turn in an uncompleted test without bargaining for a bit more time. If you do have a little time left after you have finished, for God's sake reread your paper! You'll find some mistakes if you have time to proofread your test, mistakes that your instructor will find for you if you don't find them first. There is something sickening for me as a professor when a student walks up to the desk a half hour or forty-five minutes into a two hour examination period and puts her completed exam on my desk. I know it's too soon. I want to ask, "Did you reread your exam? Is there a question you left blank? Was there another question that was unclear to you? Did you get stuck somewhere?

A lot of the time your instructor will be willing to help you if you run into a snag during a test, but he can't help you if you don't ask. If you turn that paper in early and head for the door, nobody can help you. ASK!

CHAPTER SIX

Term Papers and Libraries

For me, the scariest and most paralyzing thing about college was writing term papers. You may not believe that, coming as it does from a professor, but I know it's true. Why? One of the things that scared me was the library. How was I supposed to find some topic in that huge mass of small drawers, each one of them filled with about a million index cards. Libraries for me are like giant unfriendly churches. I feel guilty and small inside them. I am allergic to dust too.

Besides the prospect of having to go into a library, the merciless one who assigns the term paper often says things like: "I am expecting some really original work" or "I want your paper to be a real contribution to the field."

I still get angry when I hear professors talk like that to undergraduates. Half the time the prof himself has never made a real contribution to his field, and yet he has the gall to ask that of undergraduate students. In the process a good number of the students get scared out of their wits, so scared that they run down the dorm hall to find out where they can buy a term paper. Out the window goes a birthday present for your mom or a new coat. You spend your hard earned money to get somebody else to write a term paper that won't be any more a contribution to the field than the one you might have done. You lose the money, and of course, you don't learn a damn thing except to be even surer that you yourself couldn't possibly write a term paper.

Now, let's tell the truth. You are not going to make a contribution to the field, whatever the field is. You might, however, learn something yourself. Who cares if somebody else learned that same thing five years ago or ten years ago or a thousand years ago? The point is for *you* to learn rather than becoming the next Nobel Prize winner in English or Business or Communications. You don't have to be a genius to write a term paper.

One of the best ways to get over the conviction that you couldn't possibly write a paper is to pick a topic that you yourself are curious about, something that interests you. That brings up the library, of course. Maybe your soul will turn to ice at the thought of all those stacks of books and all those people behind desks that have that look of knowing so much they couldn't possibly bother with someone as dumb as a poor undergraduate.

Well, what to do? It is helpful for me to remember that I don't need to know everything about any library. All I need is four or five references for my paper. Incidentally, professors *do* still write term papers. They are required for us to get ahead in our fields. We call them articles and have them published in scholarly journals. Most of them are no more original than your term papers. Well, back to the point, how do you tackle the library?

As I mentioned earlier, you don't have to tackle it all, just a small part. I really think the best way to learn about a library is piece by piece, as you need to know. Most librarians don't know *all* about the libraries they work in. How to learn the small part of the library that has what you are looking for in it? Ask for the reference librarian. Describe your project and request his help. You will probably be amazed to discover that those forbidding people in horn-rimmed glasses *do* want to help you. Within the last year I very hesitantly asked a reference librarian about finding a book. He looked amused at my bashfulness and pointed out that his job was to help people like me. His very words were, "Frank, this is why we are here!"

You will need to have cut your question down to size when you approach one of those forbidding people, so that you won't ask a question so vague as to make it impossible for anybody to help you.

Suppose you are interested in terrorism. The interest part is good, but the topic is too broad. How about "Italian Terrorism in the Nineteen Eighties" or "Terrorism on the Airlines." Narrow your question down.

When your friendly librarian indicates to you a number of book chapters or magazine articles, you must remember that you can drown in these things. There can be so many of them on so many different aspects of your topic as to give you an immediate headache and a strong desire to climb up on the roof of the library building, bid a heartfelt goodbye to all research, and jump off.

Four or five references are plenty! After you have dug around for a while, pick four or five that you like, read them thoroughly and outline them. By the time you get to know your references well, you'll probably have a line on what you want to say. The next thing to do is write a short outline of what you want to say. Something like this, for example:

Italian Terrorism in the Nineteen Eighties

I. Who are the terrorists?
   A. General description
   B. Some specific groups of note
II. How they operate
   A. Kidnapping and ransom, assassination, torture and crippling
   B. Two famous examples
III. Combatting terrorism
   A. Early unsuccessful efforts
   B. What the police learned
   C. Later techniques
      1. Bribing captured terrorists
      2. Rewarding those who inform on others by means of judicial immunity
      3. Patience and the use of still penalties against those who won't cooperate

IV. Conclusion

When you have an outline, it is time to write. Don't get sidetracked by new ideas, don't worry about misspellings or bad sentences. Write! and keep writing until you get all the way to the end. Use plenty of examples as you go. When you have got to the end, if there's time, stick the whole thing in a drawer for a day or two, even a week. You will be sick of it. After letting it sit a little, get it out, read over it, check spellings and sentences, add a bit here or there. Get someone to check the correctness of your spelling or grammar if you can. Then type it and hand it in. None of these operations requires a genius. Writing a term paper requires only that you can find an interesting topic, the nerve to ask for help in the library, and not taking your instructors too seriously when they ask you for original work and "real" contributions.

As a parting hint to the prospective term paper writer, I would advise putting down what you have to say in your own words. Just copying out what someone else says, especially if you don't footnote, is not good writing, it can be spotted by experienced readers, AND it makes your work uneven. Taking what other people say is fine, but put the body of your work in your own words. You'll earn more doing it that way and your paper will be smoother. Plagiarizing is another word for bad writing.

It is time to close this chapter. Again, at the end, it is good to ask the question, "What if I finish my paper late?" My advice is, "Never give up. Ask for an extension. Make up a wild story, if you have to, but try to get your prof to accept your paper late. Most students give up too soon in their efforts to get late papers accepted. Push!"

CHAPTER SEVEN

God, Buddies and Mentors

The last three chapters of this book have concerned them selves with basic collegiate study skills. They are filled with the bric a brac of getting organized in classroom and place of study. Some of you may have found these chapters helpful, but I want you to know that I am aware that chapters such as those can get very dry and heavy. All these techniques! There seems to be no end of skills required. Too much talk about skills can be horribly and lethally boring. This chapter is not about skills. It's about some basic common problems that don't have a lot to do with making outlines or using the library.

Have you stopped to think that when you left your home and hometown that one of the things that got to be very much up for grabs was your religious beliefs? I'm guessing that you have run into a wide variety of belief and unbelief here at college. Some of you will have found that variety upsetting. I want to remind you here that this whole book is addressed to people who have *not* found the answers to various questions that are commonly important to college students. If religious belief is no issue to you, you won't get much out of this part of this chapter.

Has it happened to you that you have discovered how little you are sure of in your own religious tradition? Do you wonder if the whole religion of your childhood may be just superstition, not worthy of an adult? If you have questions like these, I'm talking to you. I personally believe that one can be a religious person without being simpleminded. I furthermore believe that if you don't question your own religious upbringing, you will never be a mature religious person. Put in different terms, I fervently believe that nobody ever went to hell for trying to be honest about what she believed. University life is an invitation to honesty in many areas of life, and religion is one of those areas.

41

One of the hardest things for any religious person to accept is the realization that there are other people who don't see it your way, other people who are just as good and just as sincere and honest as you are. Pushing the matter further, it is hard to believe that there is more than one chosen people. Let me be specific.

I grew up in a household that was solidly Roman Catholic, everyone that is, except my mother. We kids prayed for years that she would see the light and join us in what we regarded as the one, true Church. We didn't exactly think she would not be saved if she persisted in being the vaguely Protestant non-church goer that she was. It was just that we were sure we were the only really true church among all the Christian churches. Other churches were seen by us as having a part of the truth, but we had it all. And, it must be said, Jews and pagans were a sort of mystery to us. Nobody ever told us that those outside the Christian churches weren't going to make it, but we knew that they were mysteriously marginal people that one hoped to baptize if possible.

Doesn't that seem quaint? And yet it goes deep. I suspect most religious children feel that their way is either the only way to God or clearly the best way. After all, for kids, the world is made up of good guys and bad guys. Those who aren't good guys are bad guys of some sort.

It's only when you start to grow up that you realize that we live in a complicated world where it is often very hard to tell the good guys from the bad guys. Most good guys have a lot of bad guy in them. There are very few guys so bad as to have no tinge of goodness. We learn that our friends have faults, that our parents have faults too, that even the greatest heroes have feet of clay.

One of the tough things to learn is that our own churches can be good places and still have bad flaws. There aren't any churches with only good people in them. There are hypocrites among every body of religious and irreligious people. If there is a church where all the people are good, I have never been there.

I believe it is the task of college students to find a church or a way of arranging their ultimate values not so much on the basis of being the one, true way of looking at things, but because they are at home there and that they find good people there. If you spend your time looking for The Perfect and the Only True Church, you'll never find it. I ask you to think about that.

Closely allied to the problem of church is the problem of God. I don't think you can ever be a mature believer in God if you don't question and search. The security of your childhood's belief ends in adolescence. You can choose to remain a child in your belief in God, but I would regard that as a sad thing, because you are striving to be an adult in the rest of your life. Questioning is the beginning of mature belief in God.

A very good question might be, "Where do I go to investigate my beliefs?" One of the prime places, of course, is your college dorm or living quarters. You don't need me to tell you that. There can be endless, heated, and impassioned discussions about the presence or absence of God in today's world. It can be very disturbing to find out that your otherwise acceptable roommate is an agnostic or an atheist or someone who simply isn't concerned.

As I sit here at the typewriter I wonder if the reader of these words will think that I can tell you just where to find the answer? I have to wryly answer that I have no such answer to give you.

What I do have to tell you is that I believe none of us knows a whole lot about God. We live in a pragmatic, hard-nosed society that wants to measure things to see if they are real. Measuring God isn't much use. I remember a little girl who was sent up to wash her hands before supper. Her mother told her washing would get the germs off her hands. While she was washing up in the bathroom the little girl said aloud to herself, "Jesus and germs, Jesus and germs! The grownups are always talking about 'em but you never see 'em!" Indeed, it is like that.

One place to look for God, of course, is in the course offerings at your university. I remember very clearly setting out to find God as a philosophy major long ago. I felt sure philosophy would let me know if, when, and how God was present in the world. I did learn that there are a lot of philosophies and that there are even more philosophers. I found a philosopher for every notion of God's presence or absence I had ever dreamed of and dozens more I had never dreamed of. I did find that one could make a good case for the existence and presence of God. Perhaps that is worth knowing. What I didn't find was

God, just a lot of reasoning about Him, or Her, or It. Universities tend to be the shrines of logic, whether philosophical logic or religious logic or scientific logic. I have not found logic a very good tool for getting in touch with God. I doubt that you will either.

You know, there are human abilities other than cold logic, although we don't feature them in colleges. I'm referring to intuition, imagination. I'm thinking of the strange ability to see that poets and artists have. I suspect that you will have a much more fruitful search for God in the world of poetry and music than in the world of logic and reason. I suspect as well that you will have a far better chance for getting in touch with God by looking within yourself than by looking outside.

You will remember that there is an early chapter in this book about keeping in touch with your deep self while you are at college. That chapter is all about places and times in which you can find peace and quiet within yourself. Although I didn't say so in the chapter, I think those very places and times; I think those same activities in which you get in touch with your deepest self are the very ones that will bring you into contact with your God. I believe that your quiet times and activities are the ones most apt to help you in your search.

It is no surprising thing for anyone to notice, as the little girl I mentioned earlier in this treatment noticed, that everybody talks about God but you never see or hear Her, or Him, or It. I think one of the reasons we don't see or hear is because we lead terribly busy and terribly noisy lives. It is as though having ears to hear and eyes to see depends on a certain interior quiet. It is the poet Gerard Manley Hopkins who said: "The world is charged with the grandeur of God." But if all your food is fast food, if all your days are rushed days, if all your study is cramming, there will never be enough silence in your life to hear or see the grandeur of God within yourself or the beauty of God's voice without.

There is another way of saying this. It lies in saying that the best road to God is the road to friendship. You don't reason your way to becoming friends with someone, even if reason does play a part in sizing up a potential friend. You make friends by meeting people, by giving them time to meet you, by giving them quality time after you meet them. You get to know your friends by spending time with them, quality time. Friendship is a leisurely process; it has its own slow rhythm. You have to give it time. You can't make friends with someone who is busy all the time; we've all tried that.

What I'm suggesting here is that the language of human friendship is a very good language to use when one is searching for God. The language of friendship is not the language of the classroom, normally; one doesn't reason to a friend. One is open and receptive. One is welcoming and vulnerable and patient. These are qualities that make for friendship. These are attitudes people who want to have friends must cultivate. Friendship itself is a gift, but you can be ready for it.

I think that a belief in God is a gift too, but one can be receptive and quiet and ready. Centuries ago Teresa of Avila spoke these words with regard to a search for God:

> What the soul must do during times of quiet amounts to no more than proceeding gently and noiselessly. What I call noise is running about with the intellect looking for many words and reflections... The will calmly and wisely must understand that one does not deal well with God by force.

And so, what I have to say to you about a search for God suggests that you look to your intuitions and hunches rather than to the learning of philosophers. I suggest you read the poets and listen to the songs rather than poring over books. I suggest that your best times for meeting God are your quiet times; the best places your quiet places; the best activities your quiet activities. If there is a language most suited to a meeting between you and God, it is the language of friendship.

It seems obvious to me but I want to be clear about it, that a chapter on God belongs very much in a book about surviving in college. Survival always is related to trust and hope. A sense for a divine presence in your life can be the rock bottom of your hope, the fundament of your trust.

You may have been wondering how any book on getting along anywhere could go so long without a treatment of friends. I think some talk about friends fits right here, since I have just told you that I think that the language of friendship is a good one to use when a person is looking for God.

You don't need me to tell you that friends are basic to survival anyplace. I bet if I asked you to describe the worst time of your life, that bad time would have been a time when you were lonely and without your buddies.

Coming up with something helpful to say about friendship is perilous business. I know that. But friends are a vital area in college life, too important to leave out of a book like this. I don't have any pat answers; I need to tell you that. What I have to say comes mostly from my own experience of friendship rather than from some theory or other.

To begin with then, one thing I don't believe is that the gregarious people, the ones who meet others easily are the ones who always have good friends. Friendship runs deeper than just being able to meet people well. I think there's a sort of stereotype built up on a group of people around a campfire drinking Miller beer and telling jokes that is evidence that most people think the "popular" ones are the people who have a gift for friendship. Some of my own best friends don't talk very much and are terrified of crowds. I don't want to be trite when I say that deep people are frequently shy and at the same time make the best of friends.

People who are my friends are the people who are willing to let me into their lives. I'm not sure they have anything else in common. It takes time to be somebody's friend; you can't hurry it. You have to be ready, but you can't go out and make a friend the way you'd go out to get a turkey for Thanksgiving dinner. You can't buy friends. Making friends is more like fishing than it is like hunting. When you go fishing you have to wait a lot at a good place to fish; some days the fish don't bite. You have to keep coming back. Usually when you get a bite, it surprises you and even scares you. Friendship is like that. It sneaks up on you. There is always an element of that surprise. Because of that element I think of friendship as a gift. I have to be there to receive it, but there is something free about it that I can't make happen.

If there is another stereotype I don't like about friendship it is the notion that you must somehow be beautiful or handsome to have friends. It's like saying that fat people can't have friends. People with warts or birthmarks surely can't have any friends. People with acne are out...no skinny people. No chance for you if you can't make witty conversation or if you sweat a lot. You should be able to play basketball and dance...you better know what's in in the world of music, and of course, however you do it, you have to be cool.

You might as well require everyone to have a Ph.D. to be eligible for friendship! I can tell you, a Ph.D. doesn't help.

What then? You have to be willing to be friends without being too picky. I honestly can't think of any other absolute requirement.

A sad aspect of American life among men in their middle years, well documented by Daniel Levinson and George Vaillant, is that most of them have no friends. The competitive world most adult males live in teaches them to regard almost everyone as a potential competitor. The fast pace of adult manhood makes the leisurely business of making and keeping friends a kind of luxury. It almost seems as though the more successful a man is in his career, the fewer friends he has.

I puzzled for years about the two men I knew of my father's contemporaries who had the most friends and were closest to their families. One of them had an emotional crackup in his thirties; the other one was known far and wide as "Lazy Lucas." He worked just enough to get by. We kids knew them both better than my father's other friends because they had time for us. I always knew where I could get a beer or two on a Sunday afternoon at the Lucas home, and I never called up before hand to ask myself over either. Neither of these men were very successful; both of them had marvelous old ages, because they had been about the business of cultivating friends and family for years before retirement. I don't have to tell you that their hot shot contemporaries, the ones who made the most money, didn't have friends and were lost in old age. This is not meant to be a book about middle-aged men, but you know all middle age is the outcome of what you decided was important when you were younger.

Even in college you can put friendship on the back burner to social success, academic success, or some form of doing the cool thing.

I would like to make a pitch here for allowing yourself to think of friends without thinking of your own age group. Another unwritten law of American life seems to be sticking with people your own age for your friends.

Older friends can be immensely helpful on a college campus

or in any school situation. They can provide a kind of inspiration special to their being older and more knowledgeable. Let's see if I can show you what I mean.

How well I remember Doctor Sibley who taught me science in the eighth grade. I used to come early to school most days, riding on my bicycle. When I got to school I'd make a beeline for Doc's lab, where he quartered all sorts of living things besides the usual paraphernalia of chemicals, bunsen burners, and all sorts of glass tubes and beakers. Doc had a live alligator in a large zinc plated tank and the alligator often escaped during the night by pushing himself up on his tail over the two foot sides of the tank. Doc and I wrestled that 'gator back into his tank on many a morning; you had to be careful too, because that nasty old lizard was nearly four feet long! I realize that handling alligators isn't everyone's cup of tea, but I was fascinated and excited to work for Doc. I took care of his guinea pigs and white rats, helped clean up the water the alligator got on the floor and just generally acted as a gofer for Doc. In exchange I won his friendship; he talked about all sorts of things that interested me, how the brine in a refrigerator cooled things off, how the air brakes worked in a train car, what mice did when they ran short of oxygen, just to name a few. Doc was the first teacher I remember who called me by my first name in a special way. He called me Frank, which would have horrified my mother, who insisted on Francis, and was different from my friends who called me Monk. That name was a bond between Doc and me; it was a special name for me and I knew that we two were friends. My science grade that year was my best grade. With another Doc Sibley or two in my early school life I know I would have wound up some sort of scientist.

I had mentors in high school too, an old priest who taught freshman algebra and used to walk out to our house to visit in the summer; he could beat any kid in the school at shooting pool. He had a thick German accent and a gruff manner, but he loved the kids in freshman Algebra and we knew it. I remember my boxing coach, too, Tony DeFilio, who treated me like a son, and my godmother who sent me presents at Christmastime and on my birthday from far off Cambridge, Massachusetts, where she was an editor for the publishing house, Houghton Mifflin. Years after my high school days she encouraged me to write and wrote detailed comments on any piece of writing I sent her.

All of these people had a special place in my life. They were adults outside my family who regarded me as a special person and they helped me to find myself at some kind of work. Some were connected with studies; others with sports; the most important one with writing.

You'll notice that I have called them mentors, older friends outside family who care for you and put you to work at something that challenges you. You have had mentors in your life too. I invite you to think back over your grade and high school years recalling the people who cared for you and who challenged you. The memory will remind you how important such people are. It is my strong suspicion that without some mentor or other, few of you would be in college today.

This treatment of mentors, however, is not meant just to recall friends from your past, no matter how important they may have been to you. I am writing this description primarily to remind you that there are potential mentors in college too. Because university life is generally so much more impersonal in the classroom, I think students who seek mentors will have to take the initiative to some extent themselves. If you take a shine to a professor, get up your nerve and go to see her or him outside class time. Not every visit to a prof will lead to the kind of friendship I'm describing, but such contacts can be very useful in getting a line on good teachers, understanding things in class you didn't get the first time through, or asking how to review for the midterm exam. There are a thousand ways professors can be useful to students outside of class; maybe you'll find an important person among your profs who will be part of something that goes beyond the semester. Having a friend on the faculty can be a marvelous experience and a great help in the business of surviving on campus.

So, there's more than one kind of friend; I use the example of professor friends, mentors. The richness of different kinds of friends goes far deeper than that. It isn't easy to write about, being venturesome in your choice of friends. It's as though everyone knows that birds of a feather flock together. Generally speaking your friends will be people who are like you. We all know that, but there's something else not as well known.

I'm thinking of certain friends who call out something deep inside of you. I'm thinking that friends like this may well be people who are not at all like you. They may be people whom your other friends won't like; they may be people your family wouldn't like either. They may be people from other countries or from a social class different from your own. They may be very unlikely people.

I remember meeting a guy my freshman year in college who was the strongest kid I'd ever met. He talked with a Texas twang and grew up in a house with his two brothers and an old servant; neither his mother nor his dad lived in that house. I'd never met anybody like that—a Texan who raised himself, strong as Paul Bunyan, full of all sorts of crazy ideas. He was an unlikely friend; my life has never been the same since meeting him. Even though I haven't seen him in twenty-five years, he is still with me.

Is there somebody like that in your life? Has there been? I'm bringing up an unlikely friend from my own life's story because I think that the unlikely ones are sometimes the best. If you are too careful to have the right kind of friends, the acceptable ones, you'll miss out on something.

Really deep people are often not very conventional; there's no special place for searching them out; you could bump into a deep person who jars your sense of what is acceptable, almost anywhere. What I'm groping for here is asking you not to run too fast if you are attracted to someone who pushed you into deep water, whose ideas are different from yours, whose sense of right and wrong challenges yours and scares you. These are sometimes the very best of friends; surely one of the reasons is that when you are around them, you find out things about yourself that you never knew before.

CHAPTER EIGHT

Boyfriends, Girlfriends, Love

Nobody should underestimate the importance of boyfriends and girlfriends for survival in college. In mass education it takes a long time before you will have older friends among the faculty. There are a lot more of you than there are of us. In the beginning at least, student advisers, counselors, clergy, and psychologists are remote people whom you don't know. Your parents are not around most of the time. That leaves a tremendous weight to be born by your college friends. In many ways you sink or swim in the first two years of college depending on your friends.

You may find it an odd thing for me to say here that your same sex friends can be more helpful than boyfriends or girlfriends in college. Why do I say that? The main reason is that your buddies don't ask· the same kind of emotional commitment from you that your boyfriend usually does. You don't have to worry about falling in love or getting pregnant or being a father or the possibility of marriage. Your same sex buddies offer you a kind of safety in friendship that romantic attachments seldom have. I'm not saying this in order to push breaking up with your boyfriend or girlfriend. I'm saying it because I want you to underline what you already know. I'm saying it because somewhere in your college years you almost surely will break up with a romantic partner. If you have left all your buddies behind for romance, nobody will be around to pick up the pieces when you break up. I'm saying this lastly because I want to remind you that you are not a freak if you feel for one reason or another that you are not ready for romance right now. Romance is a two-edged sword in college; it can cut you to shreds, you know. Strictly in terms of getting on with your schooling, buddies are safer and they usually last longer than romantic partners.

On the other hand, we both know that it happens all the time that a romantic partner, a boyfriend or girlfriend can be the rock to which you cling in your early college years. I'm not knocking it. There's no doubt that many college students are sustained by a romantic partner right through school. Your loved one can provide an ear for your troubles, a shoulder to cry on, a person who helps you see that after all you do have something going for you when you don't see it by yourself.

Whoever it was who said that one of the most important characteristics of young love is long conversations was surely right. Those long all nighters, those long afternoons and evenings, those horrendously expensive telephone conversations are a vital means whereby you get to know yourself. Who can underestimate the great power of a friendly ear? I really think that finding yourself in college has as much to do with long conversations as anything else. Certainly they are as important as anything that happens in the classroom or in your reading and writing. A lot of the time, your partner in those long conversations is your loved one, your romantic partner.

We both know, by the way, that you can have a buddy who is a woman when you are a man. You can have a buddy who is a man when you are a woman. You can be just friends. Sometimes you will have people your own age you have known from childhood who are in that category, good friends of the opposite sex who are just good friends without romance. For the purposes of this book, they come under the heading of buddies. I might add, and maybe you have had this experience also, that buddies sometimes turn into lovers, and *that* is the beginning of another story.

We both know as well that there are gay men and women on campus, people whose romantic friendships are among same sex friends. By and large, gay people have the same helps and problems with romantic love that the straight folks have. Romantic joys and sorrows have much in common whatever your sexual preference is. It is those common things that concern me most here.

So much for clarification about lovers. How about *making* love? Any challenges there? Of course there are.

To begin with, sex, to quote Robertson Davies, is healthy, like eating yogurt or playing tennis. It *can* be safe, since the advent of effective contraception. There's no doubt in my mind about the healthiness of sex or the possibility of its being safe. Playing baseball is healthy too and reasonably safe if you wear a batting helmet. If you practice a lot, you can get good at it. The question arises, maybe if you practice making love a lot, you can get good at that as well. I believe that too. It would seem that the sexual taboos of your mothers and grand- mothers, many of whom thought of sex as dirty and all of whom thought of it as dangerous, could be swept out the door like last week's dirt.

But how about that feeling of being used? What is it to be seen as a mere sexual object by your partner? Nobody likes to be used; I don't and you don't. If I have a caution about today's sexual liberty, my caution would be in that area. It's as though a beautiful and a good thing can be cheapened by separating it from love. It isn't possible to make deep love with someone you don't know or care for. You can get to be very good at tech- niques, but you are inevitably faking the love part of making love if you are an indiscriminate lover. The multiplication of sexual intimacies doesn't add up to friendship or the kind of intimacy that friendship implies. There isn't any surer sign of a lonely person that one who is an indiscriminate lover. Indis- criminate lovers are not deeply concerned with their partners. I suppose the surest way to learn this is to be used sexually by somebody else, someone you thought you cared for. I'd be a fool if I asked you to take my word for all this, because I am old and you are young. What I am asking you to do is to learn from your own sexual experience; when the writing is on the wall, pay attention to it.

We live in a time when it is very cool to be experienced sexually. For some reason the cool ones won't tell you about that feeling of being used or that good love making is reserved for good friends. If it is a let down to find out your lover was using you, it is a sort of pathetic sadness to find out that your lover was making love in order to be cool.

I feel diffident about advising you about love between friends. Couples sleeping together during the college years is commonplace. My concern centers around knowing that love making is special and beautiful. Sleeping with someone who is very concerned about you can be a beautiful thing; the inti- macy of such a friend can be an immense support in your life at college. It may lead to marriage, but most of the time couples who sleep together in their undergraduate years break up before marriage. If it was the task of your grandmothers and grandfathers to discover that sex was beautiful and good, I think it is your task two generations later to be very discriminating about how you use this beautiful thing.

How about marriage itself? I've learned a lot from my own female students on this score. Most of them are very reluctant to discuss marriage until they get their careers squared away. Many of them had mothers who quit college to marry; those mothers often don't get a second chance to go back to school until they are in their thirties or forties. That's a big sacrifice.

Another reason for being slow to marry has to do with finding yourself. We've talked about college as a place where students are in search of themselves. To save making a permanent commitment to somebody else until you have some kind of a line on yourself makes sense. It is helpful, when choosing a long term partner, to be able to know what kind of a person you've got. That's very hard to do if your prospective partner has no idea what he's got for talent or what he is going to do with it. It's not a bad idea to wait until he gets it together, so you know what you're getting. Writing this chapter has reminded me how hard it is to write about sex and love from a positive point of view. It's much easier to say where all the danger points are in sexual love. My own conviction lies with saying that sex should go with caring. It should be evidence of a real commitment between people who are friends and who intend to stay friends.

CHAPTER NINE

Roots

When I was in my early twenties I was studying to be a Catholic priest and having a terrible time with my studies. I didn't like philosophy; I felt cooped in by all the rules and regulations and intimidated by the very intelligent young men who were my classmates. There was an old priest who lived not far from our quarters at St. Louis University, a fine scholar with a tongue as rough as a truck driver's. He had known my family all his life. When I went to him for advice, one of the things he suggested was for me to look at my aunts and uncles. He had known most of them from childhood. "They're not so different from you, Yogi," he said. (Yogi was my nickname) Almost all of them have personal characteristics like yours. Most of them are no more even tempered than you are. They've had terrible ups and downs too. And most of them have survived and are interesting people."

I was struck by his saying that because I was very down on myself. I wondered if I could ever learn all that dry philosophy that was required to become a priest. I wondered if the headaches I had would ever go away. I wondered if I would ever find something I was good at. And here was this rough old character, who knew me through and through telling me to look at my aunts and uncles....and telling me that I wasn't so different from them. I had some pretty neat relatives, nobody famous, but a lot of them I looked up to. I'd never thought of thinking that if they could survive, so could I.

Your family is not the same as mine, but you do have one and the people in it are like you in many ways. I'm going to ask you to think about them, the ones who are older and the ones who are younger too. Make yourself a list of the names of the people in your family you like the best. You may have a younger sister who is the world's neatest kid. You may have a grandmother who is special to you or a renegade uncle Joe who has always intrigued you. Write down all their names and describe each one as best you can. They are your blood relatives. Many of the good things they have you share. You may wind up with an interesting list.

I would suggest further that if there is anyone in your family that is old, you take a tape recorder the next time you go home and pay one or two of the old ones a visit. Ask each one to tell you the story of her life. You may be amazed at what you hear. These are your people; you share in their strengths, their troubles, their triumphs. Knowing about them can help you through confusing times.

The poet and dancer Maya Angelou writes in her autobiography that she made a list of what she called her allegiances when she was in high school.

> The allegiances I owed at this time in my life would have made very strange bedfellows: Momma with her solemn determination, Mrs. Flowers and her books, Bailey with his love, my mother and her gaiety, Miss Kirwin and her information, my classes of drama and dance.

These were the people who had helped and inspired a young, black woman to survive. She was smart enough to keep their names and to treasure all they stood for. Some of these people were family. "Momma" was her grandmother, Bailey her younger brother. Others were teachers and mentors, like Mrs. Flowers and Miss Kirwin.

Who are your allegiances? I've suggested you make a start with family but there will be others outside your family circle. You can add those others to your list. Describe them to yourself and write that description down. More important, keep those people alive in your mind. You can think of them any time you want to, you know. I would further suggest that some of them are people who are still available to you. Next time you get a chance to go home, go visit one or other of them. If they knew you when you were younger, if they cared for you and helped you then, there is every chance that they still know you and still care. You have the opportunity with some of them to deepen that early relationship and to make it even more valuable than it already is.

Not long ago I was talking to a friend of mine about his father. Going all the way back to his childhood he remembered his father telling him that it was his task to do better in his life than his father before him. My friend's father had driven a semi for more than thirty years. He was a truck driver. His son, as an accountant for a large business firm, has done what his father asked. He has moved up the ladder. That's a very American story, being upward bound. It brings up the business of family occupations. What your parents have done for a living has a lot to do with what you do. Not just parents, but aunts and uncles, grandparents and even remoter ancestors provide us with role models, even if we "surpass" them.

You might be surprised at the occupations of your older relatives. One of them may well have had an occupation that will provide you with inspiration for your own future. Women with working mothers or working aunts, for example, have a tremendous advantage on the job over women whose moms were housewives. Working moms can be marvelous role models for their daughters. It can be really helpful to find someone in your family who has done something careerwise that parallels your own ambitions. You may go beyond that person, but you will be standing on her shoulders.

While we're talking family as role models, there is another important category, the family characters. Almost every family has some oddballs in it, some people who don't conform, who are different. These are the people I mean by the word "character."

I had an aunt Myrtle who was a character. She was widowed before I was born, had no children, and as far as I know, never worked a day in her life. She lived on the money her husband had left her. She was in her sixties when I first knew her. She'd had her face lifted so many times that she had to paint her eyebrows on with eyebrow pencil. Her real eyebrows were halfway up her forehead. I guess she shaved them to keep them from showing. Aunt Myrtle was not at all pretty, despite the facelifts. She wore rouge and lots of bright red lipstick, drove a LaSalle convertible, and was reputed never to have shifted gears in her life. She just rammed the gears of that old car into second when she wanted to start, gunned the engine, and slowly let out the clutch. Off she went with a great roar of the engine, and she never geared up either. She could get that thing up to sixty in second speed! Aunt Myrtle couldn't be bothered with shifting gears.

On two consecutive Christmases she gave me first a set of real dueling pistols, and then a beautifully carved and painted pair of carved wooden herons. These were not ordinary presents for a boy in his early teens.

At parties she would seek out the kids and tell us stories about strange things that had recently happened to her. I remember one story about a ghost that appeared to her on a golf course. And another about a person long dead who kept appearing to her from behind the trees that bordered the grounds of her summer cottage in New Hampshire. I never had the impression that she was telling stories in order to amuse us nephews and nieces. It was more as though we were the only ones who would understand the mysterious events in her life. She told us her stories with obvious delight, her fake eyebrows rising with awe as she related about some particular ghost that had appeared to her just last week. We loved her.

And then there was my uncle John, who had twelve kids and lived in the country. I remember him driving around in a huge but very dilapidated Packard loaded with kids or food for his family. He came wheeling into our driveway one Spring afternoon, his car loaded with groceries. In the back of the car, on top of countless supplies of groceries for his brood, were a series of trays holding twelve dozen hot cross buns. Hot cross buns were a traditional sweet roll that Roman Catholics ate on Good Friday, the cross in memory of the crucifixion of Jesus. My mom had brought home a measley single dozen hot cross buns for our dinky little family that very morning. Uncle John did everything big.

When we kids went out to visit his family, there were always extra kids besides his own twelve. More kids were always welcome. I remember spending one night at his house in a large sleeping room at the top of the stairs of the ramshackle but somehow dignified house he and my aunt lived in on an old farm outside St. Louis. There were three kids sleeping at one end of the bed I was in, and three more at the other end, so that our feet met in the middle!

I remember him carving a gigantic turkey, for a Sunday

supper. There was one huge table in the center of the dining room with kids squashed together all round it, and another smaller table up against one wall which seated the kids who wouldn't fit at the big one. Each of the kids were screaming for a leg of this huge bird, and there were only two legs, of course. It was the yelling that fascinated me. My own house was quite sedate at supper. Eating at Uncle John's was like going to the circus. My uncle John was no ordinary man.

Now, there are a couple of MY family characters. They were important to me for a lot of reasons, one of which surely was that they both loved children. And I was a child when I knew them best. Another reason is that I grew up knowing that there were people in my family who were different from most other people. They were characters, but that didn't prevent them from being part of the family, and accepted as such in the family. Neither of those particular characters ever took kids aside to tell us, "See kids, you can be different too, if you want," but the lesson was there.

I'm sure there are some characters somewhere in your family or among the close adults of your childhood. If you yourself aspire to doing something different with your life, if you tend to be a bit of a maverick yourself, the family characters can be a great source of strength to you. Their example can give you permission to do what *you* want to do.

The last category I want you to take a look at in your family is the category of belief and unbelief.

Let's see if I can explain.

When I was a boy in grade school, my family went to church every Sunday. All five of us were by habit prone to being late. Not a punctual person in the tribe. And we were always late for church. Our way of handling this family proclivity was to have my mother drive the car. My father and all three kids were Roman Catholics. We were bound by our church's rules to regular Sunday attendance at what Catholics call Mass. There was a certain point in the service that you had to be present for or it didn't count. If you came in too late for that part, you had to go in search of a later service somewhere else to fulfill your obligation.

My mother was our driver for the most obvious of reasons. She wasn't a Catholic; she was not, in consequence, bound by our rules. She could come into church whenever she felt like it...or not at all. This being the case, she would drive us all to church, letting us out right in front so that we could all scurry inside in hopes of being not too late. After we were all safely out of the car, she made a leisurely search by herself for a parking place. With the car parked, she would drift over to the church building to attend whatever of the service remained unbound by the restrictions that were part of the religion of the rest of us.

From the time I started going to church, I knew that there was more than one way to handle religion! There were two different ways in my own family—my dad's way and my mother's. Even though as kids we all prayed that my mother would see the light and join the Catholic church, I knew as well that she resisted our efforts all through my childhood. And we had more than just my mother to deal with.

How well I remember one evening at home when we were all making lists of things we were thankful for, taking turns at reading our lists out loud for the edification and interest of the other family members. My mother's mother was there with us. She was a woman of great influence in our family, respected by her in-laws and really loved by her grandchildren. My grandmother read her list after several of us had read ours. My younger sister had read her list already; at the top of her items for thanksgiving was the following words: "I'm glad that I am a Catholic." There was a glint in my grandmother's eye when her turn to read came. Very distinctly she read, "I'm glad that I am an Episcopalean." There was a considerable silence that followed her words. None of us knew quite what to say. Catholics of that day did not like being reminded that there were other ways to save your soul than our way. In my family you just couldn't escape that knowledge. My mom was an agnostic; my grandmother an Episcopalean. Shocking as it was, we knew down deep, each of us kids, that there was more than one way of being religious including having no affiliation at all.

Now, how about you? You may well be taking a second look at your own religious convictions. We have talked about that in an earlier chapter. My point here is that you may well get some help in this matter by taking a second look at your family. Take a look at the people you respect most. It is very possible that somewhere in your family there is someone you might have overlooked whose religious convictions appeal to you now. That person may be your mother or dad. The religion that fits best may be the one you were taught as a child, but that's not necessarily so. You may take a sprinkling of another point of view from one of your aunts. You may have a renegade uncle who has no belief at all, but who is a kinder person than any of the church goers you know.

The point is that childhood's important people go very deep. It is often helpful to look at important family members in seeking your own religious answers. Your family is a rich source for models for your own life. Usually there is a variety to choose from. The older people in my family, usually without their knowing it, helped me in college. I hope that their counterparts in your family and neighbors will help you too.

CHAPTER TEN

Suffering, Identity, Freedom

If you take a look back in this book, you'll remember that we began with a cameo look at a college campus with an emphasis on its pace and the confusion that surrounds it. We took a hard look at your deep self as the rock bottom of your existence and the means you might take to stay in touch with what is deepest and most worth while in your life. We got into the practical aspects of a life of study, the bare bones. We looked, you and I, at the politics of the classroom and discussed the place of student etiquette. We talked about taking exams and writing term papers. We talked about the importance of your friends in the context of survival. In the context of friendship and solitude, we talked about mature belief and taking a new look at your church. We got into the central position of boyfriends and girlfriends in college life. Lastly we took a look at roots, specifically how childhood's important people can continue to be sources of strength and avenues of life for today and the future.

One of the things that I have assumed in an interested reader of this book has been a certain quality of not having it together. If you know exactly what you're doing, you won't have found this book interesting. I want to talk here at the end of the book about that very quality of not being together. What can you learn from the confusion? What is the confusion all about? I think you already know that just because you have read a book about surviving in college, that isn't going to get you out of a sizeable amount of pain and confusion.

There is a very real sense in which the hard part of going to college would have happened to you whether or not you decided to give college life a try. You'd have had something like what you are going through here no matter where you went after high school. College happens to be the place where you have it. As a matter of fact, what I'm talking about didn't begin

in college at all. It began in high school; it only continues in a
new and more sophisticated form in college. I'm talking about
what psychologists call the crisis of identity. Erik Erikson, who
coined the term, describes it as follows:

> It occurs in that period of the life cycle when each youth
> must forge for himself some central perspective and direc-
> tion, some working unity out of the effective remnants of his
> childhood and the hopes of anticipated adulthood; he must
> detect some meaningful resemblance between what he has
> come to see in himself and what his sharpened awareness
> tells him others judge and expect him to be.

It is in the context of this crisis of identity that I have wanted
you to look back to your childhood. Erikson says that you forge
an identity "out of the effective remnants...of childhood." This
means that you take your own childhood as the clay out of
which to mold your adult self. Childhood's best times and
places are a part of this. Childhood's important people, family
people and other people are important here too. Your childhood's religious foundation and its attitude toward a supreme
being have marked you deeply, as have the attitude toward
work you learned as a kid, and your childhood's loves. Because
of the importance of your childhood we have frequently keyed
in this book on your early days as a rich source for finding
yourself now.

You will recall that Erikson does not content himself with
childhood alone in his description of the process of youth's
forging for herself some central perspective or direction, some
working unity. He discusses as well the "hopes of anticipated
adulthood." This book is intended to help you look forward to
life after college by learning to survive well in college. Your life
of love and friendship after college will depend a lot on the
friends and loves you have in these years. Your intellectual
interests later and your life of work later will depend a lot on
your interests here. Sparks of interest here in school will shine
out in your later life over and over, regardless of the turns your
career may take. I encouraged you to put your real interests
first in the choice of a major area of study for this reason. Only
things that you find interesting will have a chance to grow later,
on and off the job.

This book has looked to your past and to your future in

terms of what is going on right now, your life in college. That is its perspective. I haven't forgotten the intent of this chapter, however, to deal with the pain involved in this hard work which you are doing here.

You'll notice that we have called these years the *crisis* of identity. A crisis is a turning point, a crucial moment when development must move one way or another. My point here is to underline that crises involve risk; they involve breaking new ground; they involve the possibility of failure. The crisis of identity on a college campus, or anywhere else for that matter, is sometimes a scary and painful process. The question we raised earlier in this chapter was simply this: what can you do with all that pain and suffering? In putting your college career in the framework of the crisis of identity, one of my points has been to make it clear that one of the things you cannot do with the painful part is to get out of it. Who hasn't, after surviving a tough year, wanted to go home and explain to a younger brother or sister, or to younger friends, all she has learned. You want to help those who come after you to avoid some of what you yourself had to endure. It's not so much that you can't help the people you care about, you can. I wouldn't be writing this book if I figured that there was nothing to be done about a crisis of identity except to endure it. It's more like saying, "I can help, but I can't do it for you." It's more like knowing that with the best help in the world each person's move from childhood to adulthood is unique. Helpful people can help all right, but there's only one you; no one else will ever quite understand.

If there is anything you can get from the inevitable growing pains attached to this crisis, I think it has something to do with compassion for others, a sense of wonder, a consolidation of strength. Viktor Frankl, a psychiatrist and survivor of the death camps of Nazi Germany, feels that suffering itself is one of the keys to finding meaning in your life. Frankl quotes the philosopher Nietzsche in saying, "Whatever does not kill me, makes me stronger." It is as though those prisoners, marked as they were with the daily possibility of dying in a gas chamber, and living with little food or clothing in the terrible Polish winters, had to reach down to the nitty gritty in a way they never had their whole lives before. They found reasons for staying alive or they died. It was as if surface living was impossible in those concentration camps. It's true, some of the prisoners became beasts, selling themselves to the Nazis to become guards of their own people, many of them becoming more brutal than the Nazis themselves. But others learned to live in a profound and loving way, reaching out beyond their terrible hardships to help their fellow prisoners.

The language of the suffering of American Blacks as told by such storytellers as Maya Angelou and Alice Walker, has a strange resonance with the writers from the death camps of Europe. Listen to Maya Angelou:

> The Black female is assaulted in her tender years by all those common forces of nature at the same time that she is caught in the tripartite crossfire of masculine prejudice, white illogical hate and Black lack of power.
>
> The fact that the adult American Negro female merges a formidable character is often met with amazement, distaste and even belligerance. It is seldom accepted as an inevitable outcome of the struggle won by survivors and deserves respect if not enthusiastic acceptance.

It is as though the author of these lines, and other American Black women like her, have emerged from prisons without walls, from death camps without barbed wire fences right here in our own country with a kind of strength they never would have had were it not for their experience of masculine prejudice, white hatred and Black lack of power.

Alice Walker, speaking in the person of Shug, in her novel, *The Color Purple,* speaks of a spiritual reawakening the rebirth of a sense of wonder. Shug says:

> Trouble do it for most folks, I think. Sorrow, lord. Feeling like shit.

What a strange way to a spiritual rebirth! Bad times, "Feeling like shit!" It is the language of survivors. If Viktor Frankl felt he learned from his terrible suffering in a camp, if Maya Angelou speaks so eloquently of her own strength born of pain, if Alice Walker mentions her character Shug's awakening as tied to "feeling like shit," I believe that your tough times in college can have the same effect on you if you want them to. It is a mysterious process, call it purification if you want, but the literature of survivors always has some voices giving evidence that out of sorrow and hardship can come depth, compassion and a new sense of wonder for the world, if you want it to.

As I'm getting close to the end of this book, it occurs to me that college is not a death camp and that there are good times there as well as times when you feel like shit.

Although survivors of the camps and people who have experienced terrible poverty, powerlessness and racial prejudice have something to tell us all, still it would be foolish to say that your school is just like Auschwitz or that you live with the daily possibility of being lynched or raped. Colleges are more civilized than that. It is possible to look at them not as prisons but as places well designed for a person to go through an identity crisis.

You know, not many people in your home town know what you are doing off there in college. Generally, your parents and friends back home know only what you want to tell them. That's a lot different from living at home. You probably don't have to live up to your home town or home school reputation either. You get a fresh start. You can try on new faces; you can try new things without someone who has known you since you were born sitting in judgement on you. You are not stuck with your old friends from back home, some of whom your family picked for you. Here at school you can pick your own friends and your own roommate. You didn't pick your roommate at home, you were stuck with your little brother, whom you didn't ask for. You just got him. There is a chance at school to study something that really interests you, to try this course and then that one with a freedom you never had in high school. Those of you who have had full time jobs at one time or another know that you have far more freedom in your work life at school than you ever have at a nine to five job. You even get to pick your own hours! You can get fired from a job in seconds. If you never went to class at all in college, it would take at least a year, probably longer to flunk out of school. To make a long story short, you are given a lot of rope in college. That can be a tremendous thrill. College can be a great place for you to slowly find yourself, because of the freedom there. I hope you come to see that. For me at least, the thing I loved the best about the college experience was my friends. When we were all thrown together, we made friends fast. That was thirty-five years ago. I still remember long evenings talking about what my friend

David Knight and I planned to do with our lives. I still remember writing crazy letters to a girl in California. I still remember playing touch football on Saturday afternoon with the ferocity of hand-to-hand combat. I still remember discovering that I could write poetry and that the college cafeteria had a bakery in back of it whose doors were unlocked, with bread still warm from the oven and with whole trays of brownies...and we never got caught. I think you will have memories that will stay with you too from these college days. And if sometimes the place does seem like a prison, there are other times when you know that it is a world all its own, a place set aside specifically for you to try new things, to do crazy things. The craziest of all is getting to know that interesting person, yourself. Good Luck!

THE END

ABOUT THE AUTHOR

Frank Gross is a professor of Social Science at Western Michigan University's College of General Studies in Kalamazoo, Michigan. He is the author of *Introducing Erik Erikson,* University Press of America, and *Passages in Teaching,* Philosophical Library. Dr. Gross has previously taught at St. Louis University in St. Louis, Missouri, and St. John's College, Belize.